Rhythm
Bootcamp

The **fastest**, most **addictive** way
to level up your **rhythm reading**

Copyright © 2014 by Philip Johnston

ISBN 978-0-9581905-7-2
Ver 1.0

Also by Philip Johnston
Not Until You've Done Your Practice (1989)
The Practice Revolution (2002)
Practiceopedia (2007)
Scales Bootcamp (2009)
The Dynamic Studio (2012)

For more help and online resources
www.insidemusicteaching.com

How to track your progress

Recording your growing list of Rhythm Reading heroics

Example only

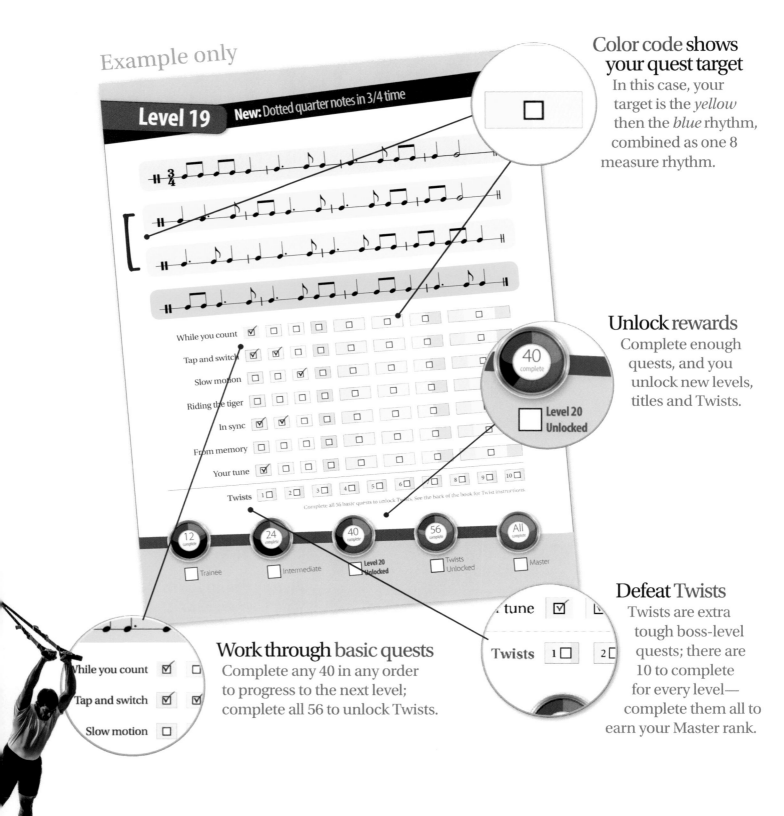

Level 19 — *New: Dotted quarter notes in 3/4 time*

While you count
Tap and switch
Slow motion
Riding the tiger
In sync
From memory
Your tune

Twists: 1 2 3 4 5 6 7 8 9 10

Complete all 56 basic quests to unlock Twists. See the back of the book for Twist instructions.

12 complete — Trainee
24 complete — Intermediate
40 complete — Level 20 Unlocked
56 complete — Twists Unlocked
All complete — Master

40 complete
Level 20 Unlocked

Color code shows your quest target

In this case, your target is the *yellow* then the *blue* rhythm, combined as one 8 measure rhythm.

Unlock rewards

Complete enough quests, and you unlock new levels, titles and Twists.

Work through basic quests

Complete any 40 in any order to progress to the next level; complete all 56 to unlock Twists.

While you count
Tap and switch
Slow motion

Defeat Twists

Twists are extra tough boss-level quests; there are 10 to complete for every level— complete them all to earn your Master rank.

tune

Twists 1 2

The basic quest requirements

Complete any 40 to unlock the next level; all 56 to unlock Twists.

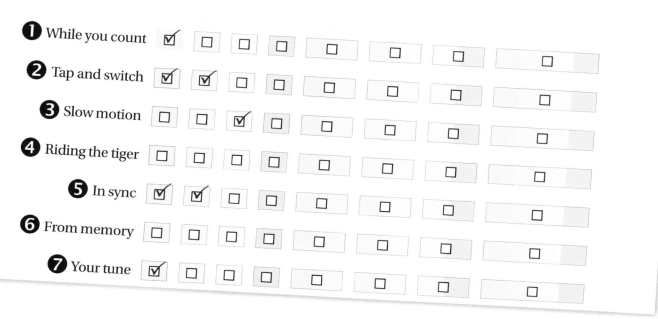

❶ While you count

Tap the rhythm while you count out loud. Tempo is up to you, as is *how* you count. (1-2-3-4...1-&-2-&-3-&-4-&...whatever helps.)

Tap and switch ❷

One hand taps the rhythm, while the other hand taps a steady beat...then you play it again, but with the hands reversing roles. Show both ways to earn the tick.

❸ Slow motion

With the metronome at just 60 bpm. Plenty of time to think, to doubt, and to have notes drifting from the underlying beat. Tougher than you think.

Riding the tiger ❹

With the metronome at 160 bpm. Make it to the end with no mistakes *twice in a row* to earn the tick.

❺ In Sync

Play the rhythm in sync with someone else—your teacher, another student, or the official recording of the rhythm at insidemusicteaching.com . (Look in the Rhythm Bootcamp section of the site)

From memory ❻

No hints, no mistakes and no music in front of you. How well do you really know the rhythm? You're about to find out.

❼ Your tune

Make up a melody for the given rhythm, play it back for your teacher to hear.

Done? Twists are next...

Once you've completed all 56 basic quests, the challenge really begins. See the **back of the book** for details of what you're in for.

Level 1

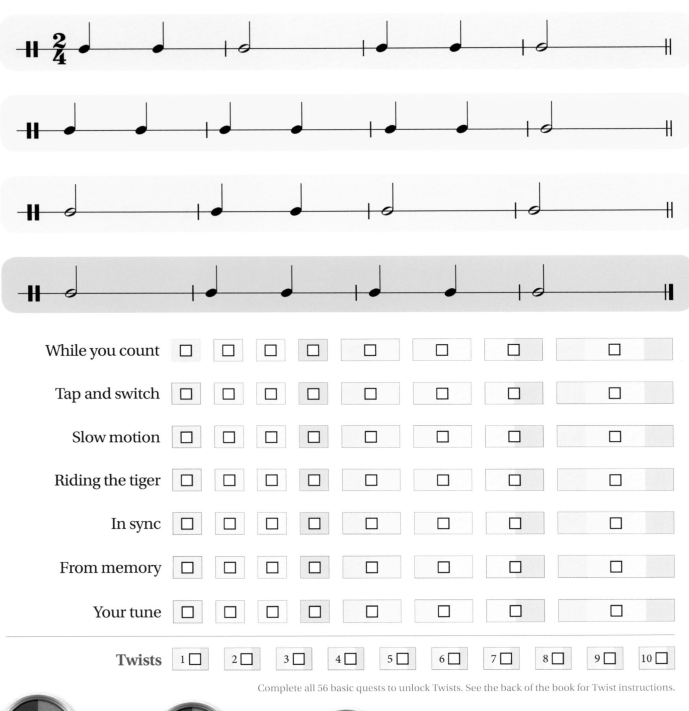

While you count	☐	☐	☐	☐	☐	☐	☐	☐
Tap and switch	☐	☐	☐	☐	☐	☐	☐	☐
Slow motion	☐	☐	☐	☐	☐	☐	☐	☐
Riding the tiger	☐	☐	☐	☐	☐	☐	☐	☐
In sync	☐	☐	☐	☐	☐	☐	☐	☐
From memory	☐	☐	☐	☐	☐	☐	☐	☐
Your tune	☐	☐	☐	☐	☐	☐	☐	☐

Twists 1☐ 2☐ 3☐ 4☐ 5☐ 6☐ 7☐ 8☐ 9☐ 10☐

Complete all 56 basic quests to unlock Twists. See the back of the book for Twist instructions.

12 complete	24 complete	40 complete	56 complete	All complete
☐ Trainee	☐ Intermediate	☐ **Level 2 Unlocked**	☐ Twists Unlocked	☐ Master

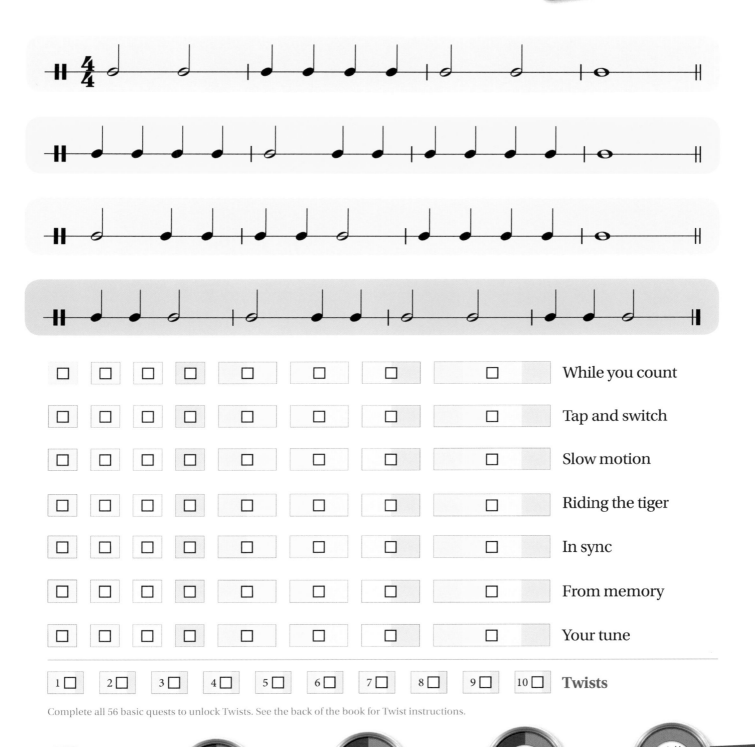

☐	☐	☐	☐	☐	☐	☐	☐	While you count
☐	☐	☐	☐	☐	☐	☐	☐	Tap and switch
☐	☐	☐	☐	☐	☐	☐	☐	Slow motion
☐	☐	☐	☐	☐	☐	☐	☐	Riding the tiger
☐	☐	☐	☐	☐	☐	☐	☐	In sync
☐	☐	☐	☐	☐	☐	☐	☐	From memory
☐	☐	☐	☐	☐	☐	☐	☐	Your tune

1 ☐ 2 ☐ 3 ☐ 4 ☐ 5 ☐ 6 ☐ 7 ☐ 8 ☐ 9 ☐ 10 ☐ **Twists**

Complete all 56 basic quests to unlock Twists. See the back of the book for Twist instructions.

12 complete

24 complete

40 complete

56 complete

All complete

Trainee

Intermediate

Level 3 Unlocked

Twists Unlocked

Master

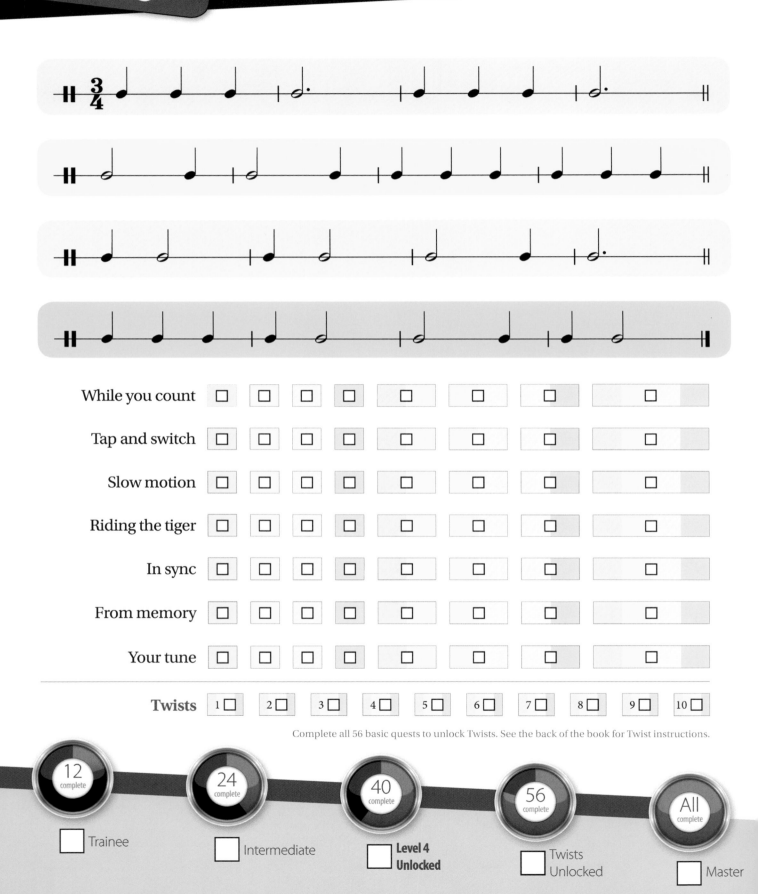

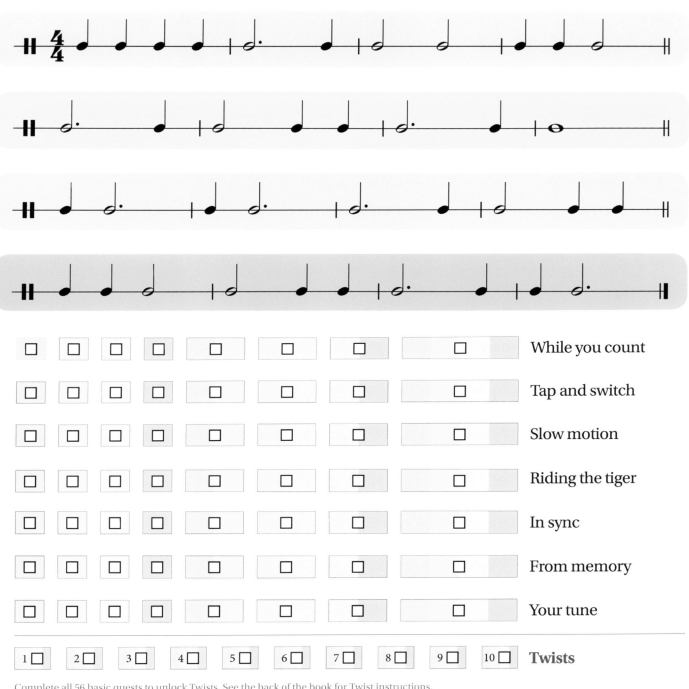

								While you count
								Tap and switch
								Slow motion
								Riding the tiger
								In sync
								From memory
								Your tune

1 ☐ 2 ☐ 3 ☐ 4 ☐ 5 ☐ 6 ☐ 7 ☐ 8 ☐ 9 ☐ 10 ☐ **Twists**

Complete all 56 basic quests to unlock Twists. See the back of the book for Twist instructions.

12 complete — Trainee

24 complete — Intermediate

40 complete — **Level 5 Unlocked**

56 complete — Twists Unlocked

All complete — Master

Level 5

New: Whole measure rests

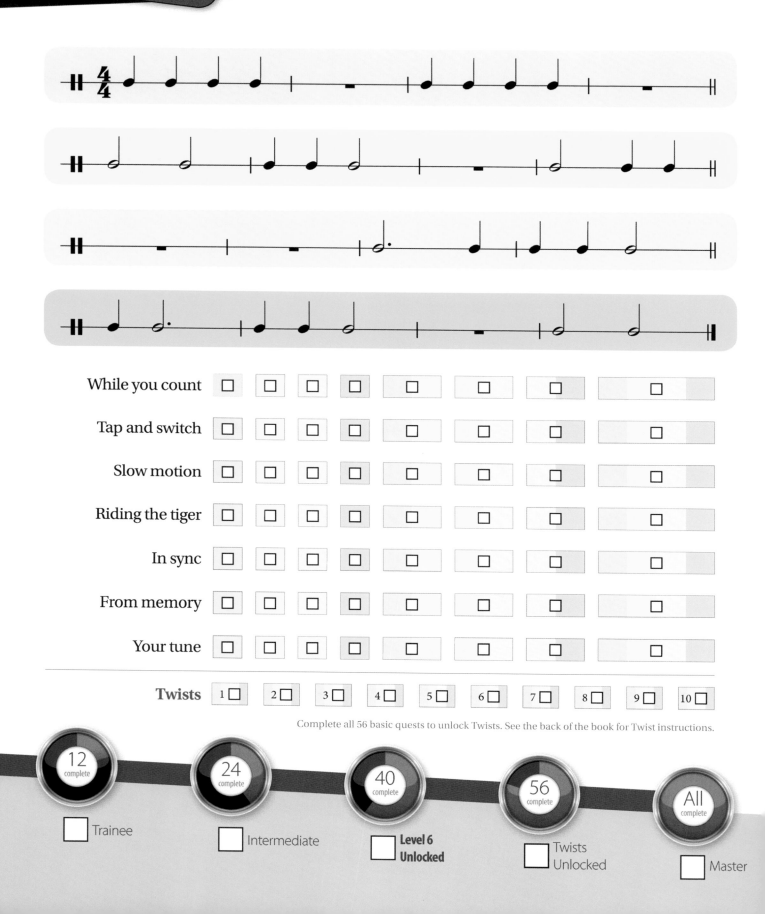

While you count	☐	☐	☐	☐	☐	☐	☐	☐
Tap and switch	☐	☐	☐	☐	☐	☐	☐	☐
Slow motion	☐	☐	☐	☐	☐	☐	☐	☐
Riding the tiger	☐	☐	☐	☐	☐	☐	☐	☐
In sync	☐	☐	☐	☐	☐	☐	☐	☐
From memory	☐	☐	☐	☐	☐	☐	☐	☐
Your tune	☐	☐	☐	☐	☐	☐	☐	☐

Twists 1☐ 2☐ 3☐ 4☐ 5☐ 6☐ 7☐ 8☐ 9☐ 10☐

Complete all 56 basic quests to unlock Twists. See the back of the book for Twist instructions.

12 complete — ☐ Trainee

24 complete — ☐ Intermediate

40 complete — ☐ **Level 6 Unlocked**

56 complete — ☐ Twists Unlocked

All complete — ☐ Master

Level 6

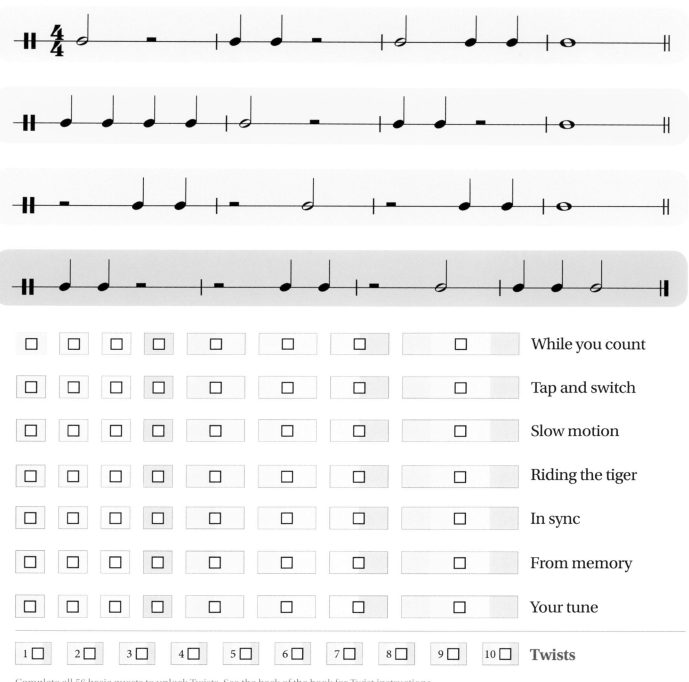

								While you count
☐	☐	☐	☐	☐	☐	☐	☐	While you count
☐	☐	☐	☐	☐	☐	☐	☐	Tap and switch
☐	☐	☐	☐	☐	☐	☐	☐	Slow motion
☐	☐	☐	☐	☐	☐	☐	☐	Riding the tiger
☐	☐	☐	☐	☐	☐	☐	☐	In sync
☐	☐	☐	☐	☐	☐	☐	☐	From memory
☐	☐	☐	☐	☐	☐	☐	☐	Your tune

1 ☐   2 ☐   3 ☐   4 ☐   5 ☐   6 ☐   7 ☐   8 ☐   9 ☐   10 ☐   **Twists**

Complete all 56 basic quests to unlock Twists. See the back of the book for Twist instructions.

12 complete

24 complete

40 complete

56 complete

All complete

☐ Trainee

☐ Intermediate

☐ **Level 7 Unlocked**

☐ Twists Unlocked

☐ Master

Level 7

New: Quarter note rests

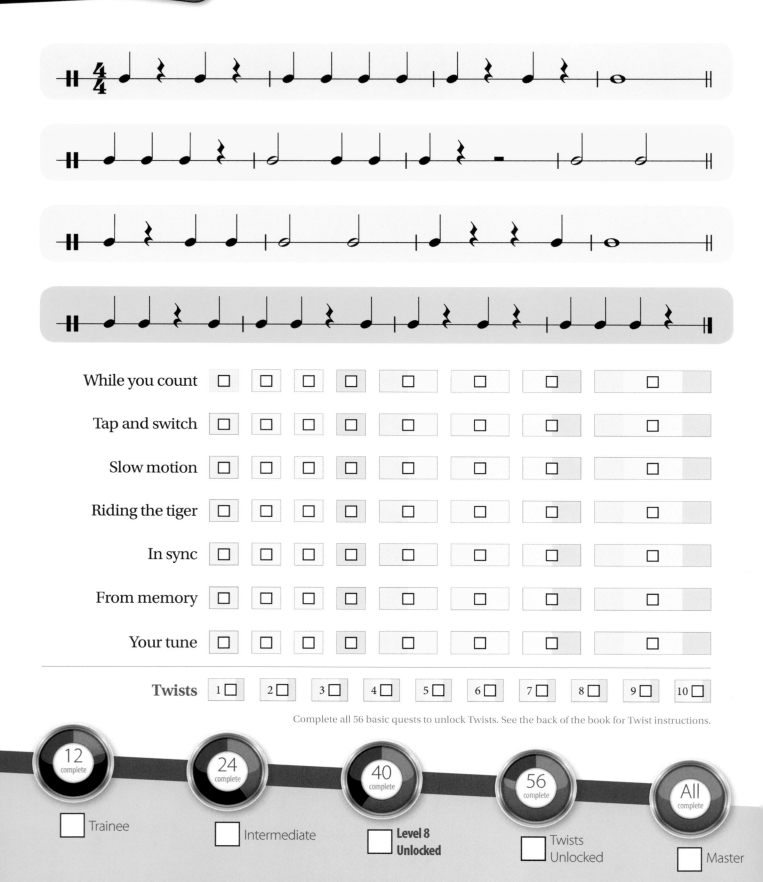

While you count	☐	☐	☐	☐	☐	☐	☐	☐
Tap and switch	☐	☐	☐	☐	☐	☐	☐	☐
Slow motion	☐	☐	☐	☐	☐	☐	☐	☐
Riding the tiger	☐	☐	☐	☐	☐	☐	☐	☐
In sync	☐	☐	☐	☐	☐	☐	☐	☐
From memory	☐	☐	☐	☐	☐	☐	☐	☐
Your tune	☐	☐	☐	☐	☐	☐	☐	☐

Twists   1 ☐   2 ☐   3 ☐   4 ☐   5 ☐   6 ☐   7 ☐   8 ☐   9 ☐   10 ☐

Complete all 56 basic quests to unlock Twists. See the back of the book for Twist instructions.

12 complete   **24** complete   **40** complete   **56** complete   **All** complete

☐ Trainee   ☐ Intermediate   ☐ **Level 8 Unlocked**   ☐ Twists Unlocked   ☐ Master

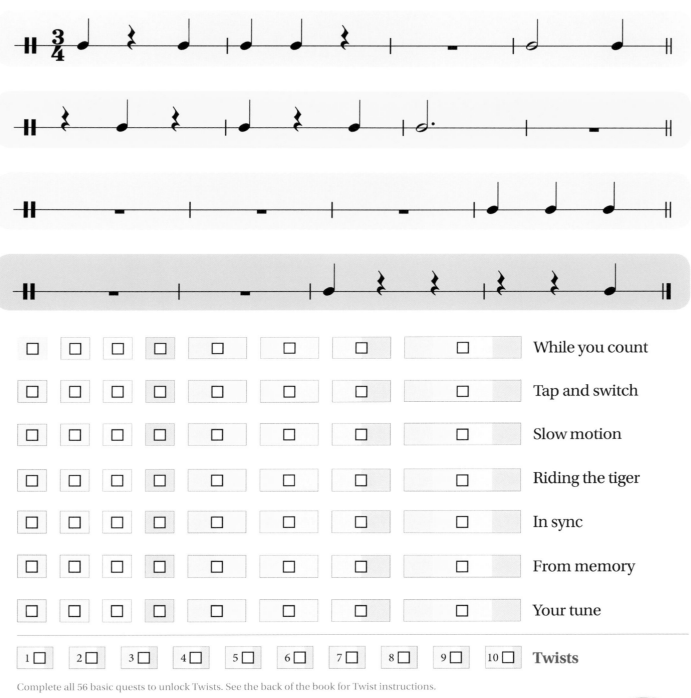

								While you count

								Tap and switch

								Slow motion

								Riding the tiger

								In sync

								From memory

								Your tune

1 ☐   2 ☐   3 ☐   4 ☐   5 ☐   6 ☐   7 ☐   8 ☐   9 ☐   10 ☐   **Twists**

Complete all 56 basic quests to unlock Twists. See the back of the book for Twist instructions.

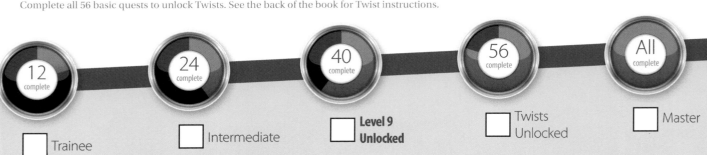

12 complete

24 complete

40 complete

56 complete

All complete

☐ Trainee

☐ Intermediate

☐ **Level 9 Unlocked**

☐ Twists Unlocked

☐ Master

Level 9

While you count	☐	☐	☐	☐	☐	☐	☐	☐
Tap and switch	☐	☐	☐	☐	☐	☐	☐	☐
Slow motion	☐	☐	☐	☐	☐	☐	☐	☐
Riding the tiger	☐	☐	☐	☐	☐	☐	☐	☐
In sync	☐	☐	☐	☐	☐	☐	☐	☐
From memory	☐	☐	☐	☐	☐	☐	☐	☐
Your tune	☐	☐	☐	☐	☐	☐	☐	☐

Twists 1 ☐ 2 ☐ 3 ☐ 4 ☐ 5 ☐ 6 ☐ 7 ☐ 8 ☐ 9 ☐ 10 ☐

Complete all 56 basic quests to unlock Twists. See the back of the book for Twist instructions.

12 complete — Trainee

24 complete — Intermediate

40 complete — **Level 10 Unlocked**

56 complete — Twists Unlocked

All complete — Master

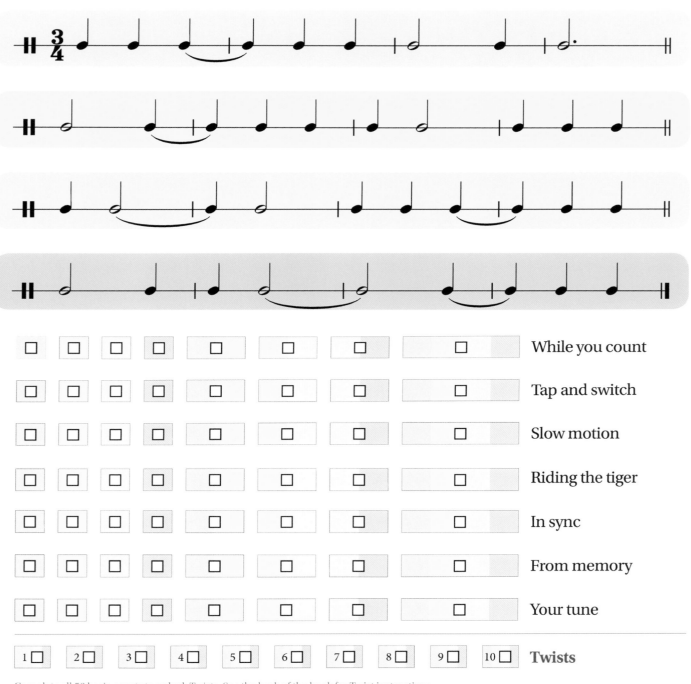

								While you count
								Tap and switch
								Slow motion
								Riding the tiger
								In sync
								From memory
								Your tune

1 ☐   2 ☐   3 ☐   4 ☐   5 ☐   6 ☐   7 ☐   8 ☐   9 ☐   10 ☐   **Twists**

Complete all 56 basic quests to unlock Twists. See the back of the book for Twist instructions.

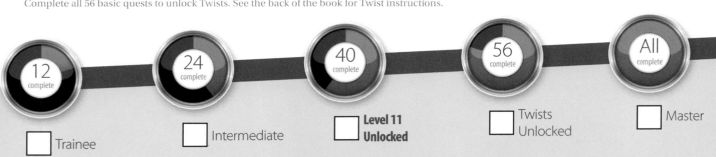

12 complete   **24** complete   **40** complete   **56** complete   **All** complete

☐ Trainee   ☐ Intermediate   ☐ **Level 11 Unlocked**   ☐ Twists Unlocked   ☐ Master

Level 11

New: Ties in 4/4 time

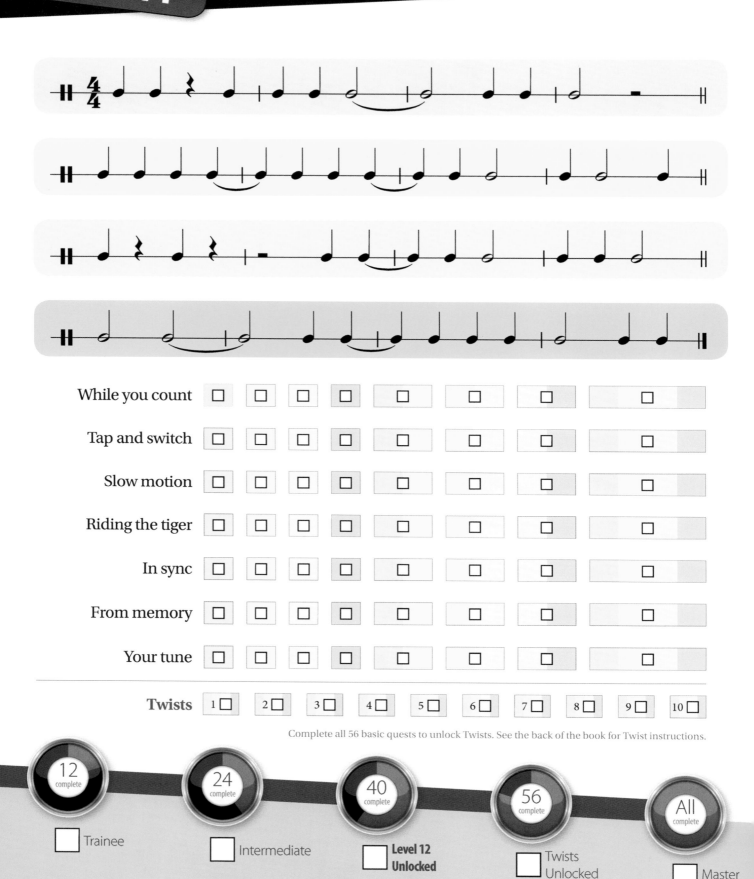

While you count	☐	☐	☐	☐	☐	☐	☐	☐
Tap and switch	☐	☐	☐	☐	☐	☐	☐	☐
Slow motion	☐	☐	☐	☐	☐	☐	☐	☐
Riding the tiger	☐	☐	☐	☐	☐	☐	☐	☐
In sync	☐	☐	☐	☐	☐	☐	☐	☐
From memory	☐	☐	☐	☐	☐	☐	☐	☐
Your tune	☐	☐	☐	☐	☐	☐	☐	☐

Twists 1 ☐ 2 ☐ 3 ☐ 4 ☐ 5 ☐ 6 ☐ 7 ☐ 8 ☐ 9 ☐ 10 ☐

Complete all 56 basic quests to unlock Twists. See the back of the book for Twist instructions.

12 complete — Trainee

24 complete — Intermediate

40 complete — **Level 12 Unlocked**

56 complete — **Twists Unlocked**

All complete — Master

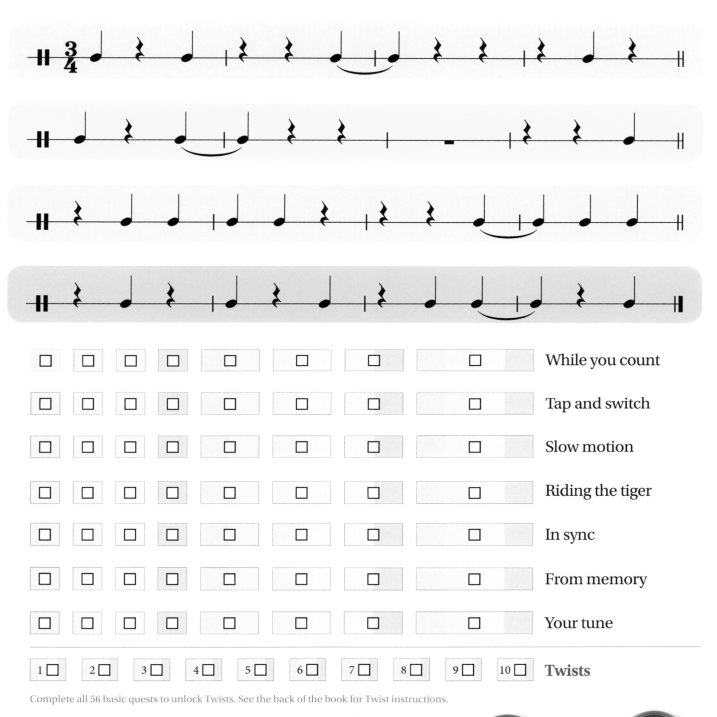

While you count

Tap and switch

Slow motion

Riding the tiger

In sync

From memory

Your tune

1 ☐   2 ☐   3 ☐   4 ☐   5 ☐   6 ☐   7 ☐   8 ☐   9 ☐   10 ☐   **Twists**

Complete all 56 basic quests to unlock Twists. See the back of the book for Twist instructions.

12 complete

24 complete

40 complete

56 complete

All complete

☐ Trainee   ☐ Intermediate   ☐ **Level 13 Unlocked**   ☐ Twists Unlocked   ☐ Master

Level 13 New: Eighth notes

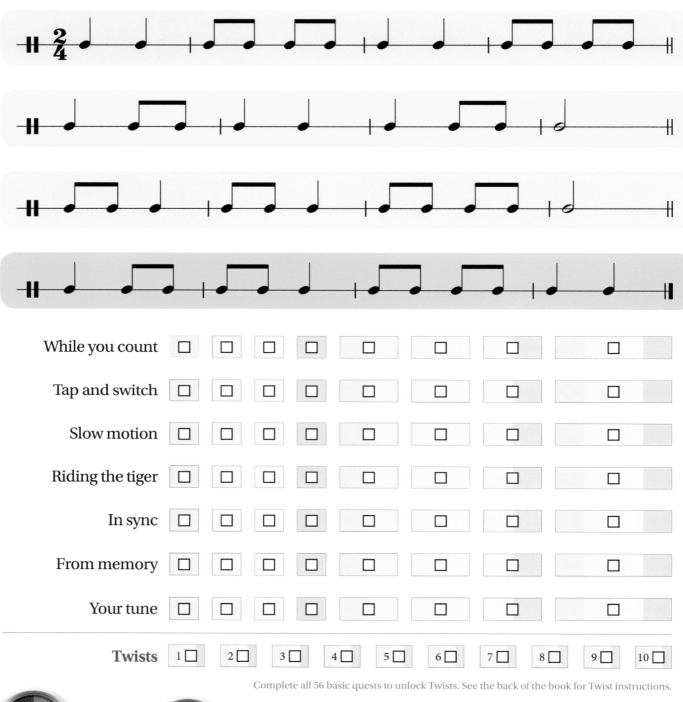

While you count	☐	☐	☐	☐	☐	☐	☐	☐
Tap and switch	☐	☐	☐	☐	☐	☐	☐	☐
Slow motion	☐	☐	☐	☐	☐	☐	☐	☐
Riding the tiger	☐	☐	☐	☐	☐	☐	☐	☐
In sync	☐	☐	☐	☐	☐	☐	☐	☐
From memory	☐	☐	☐	☐	☐	☐	☐	☐
Your tune	☐	☐	☐	☐	☐	☐	☐	☐

Twists 1 ☐   2 ☐   3 ☐   4 ☐   5 ☐   6 ☐   7 ☐   8 ☐   9 ☐   10 ☐

Complete all 56 basic quests to unlock Twists. See the back of the book for Twist instructions.

12 complete ☐ Trainee

24 complete ☐ Intermediate

40 complete ☐ **Level 14 Unlocked**

56 complete ☐ Twists Unlocked

All complete ☐ Master

Level 14

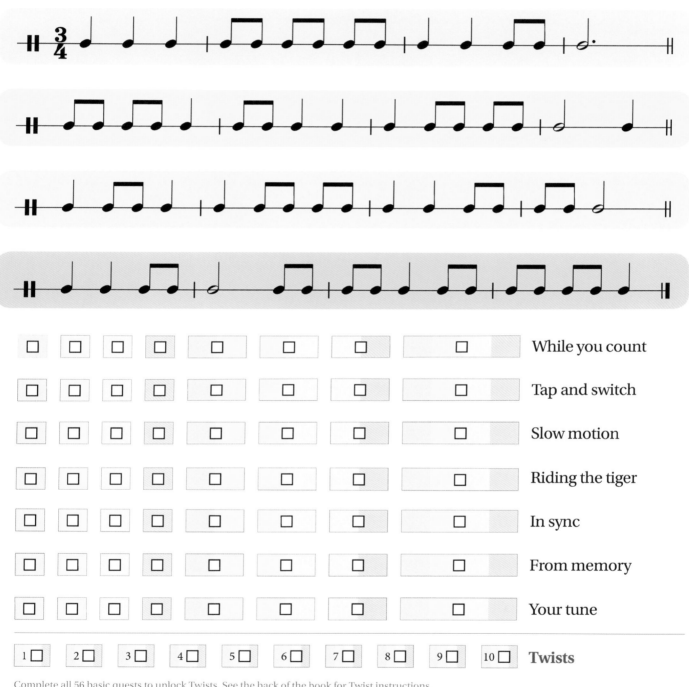

								While you count
□	□	□	□	□	□	□	□	**While you count**
□	□	□	□	□	□	□	□	**Tap and switch**
□	□	□	□	□	□	□	□	**Slow motion**
□	□	□	□	□	□	□	□	**Riding the tiger**
□	□	□	□	□	□	□	□	**In sync**
□	□	□	□	□	□	□	□	**From memory**
□	□	□	□	□	□	□	□	**Your tune**

1 □   2 □   3 □   4 □   5 □   6 □   7 □   8 □   9 □   10 □   **Twists**

Complete all 56 basic quests to unlock Twists. See the back of the book for Twist instructions.

12 complete — Trainee
24 complete — Intermediate
40 complete — **Level 15 Unlocked**
56 complete — Twists Unlocked
All complete — Master

Level 15

New: Eighth notes in 4/4 time

While you count	☐	☐	☐	☐	☐	☐	☐	☐
Tap and switch	☐	☐	☐	☐	☐	☐	☐	☐
Slow motion	☐	☐	☐	☐	☐	☐	☐	☐
Riding the tiger	☐	☐	☐	☐	☐	☐	☐	☐
In sync	☐	☐	☐	☐	☐	☐	☐	☐
From memory	☐	☐	☐	☐	☐	☐	☐	☐
Your tune	☐	☐	☐	☐	☐	☐	☐	☐

Twists 1 ☐ 2 ☐ 3 ☐ 4 ☐ 5 ☐ 6 ☐ 7 ☐ 8 ☐ 9 ☐ 10 ☐

Complete all 56 basic quests to unlock Twists. See the back of the book for Twist instructions.

12 complete — ☐ Trainee

24 complete — ☐ Intermediate

40 complete — ☐ **Level 16 Unlocked**

56 complete — ☐ Twists Unlocked

All complete — ☐ Master

Level 16

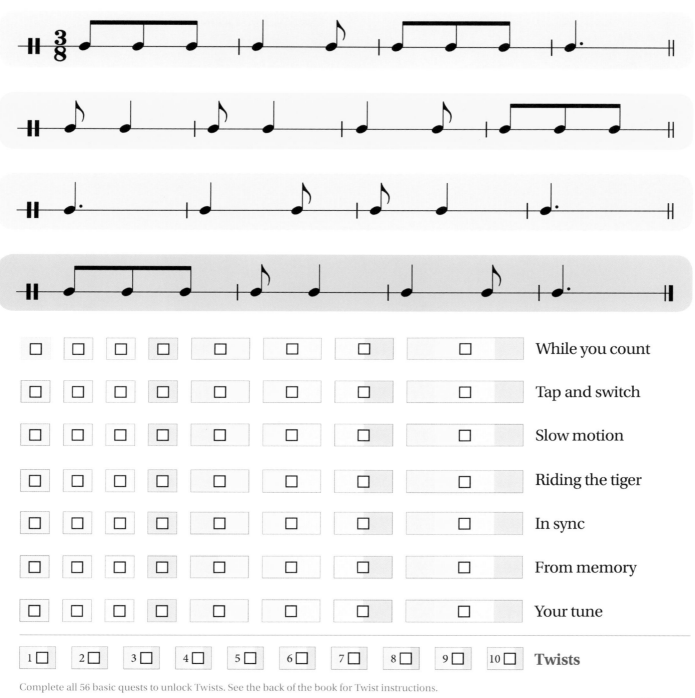

								While you count
☐	☐	☐	☐	☐	☐	☐	☐	While you count
☐	☐	☐	☐	☐	☐	☐	☐	Tap and switch
☐	☐	☐	☐	☐	☐	☐	☐	Slow motion
☐	☐	☐	☐	☐	☐	☐	☐	Riding the tiger
☐	☐	☐	☐	☐	☐	☐	☐	In sync
☐	☐	☐	☐	☐	☐	☐	☐	From memory
☐	☐	☐	☐	☐	☐	☐	☐	Your tune

1 ☐   2 ☐   3 ☐   4 ☐   5 ☐   6 ☐   7 ☐   8 ☐   9 ☐   10 ☐   **Twists**

Complete all 56 basic quests to unlock Twists. See the back of the book for Twist instructions.

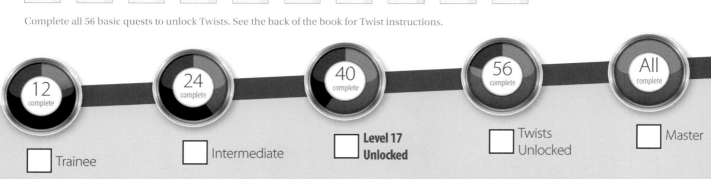

☐ Trainee   ☐ Intermediate   ☐ **Level 17 Unlocked**   ☐ Twists Unlocked   ☐ Master

Level 17   New: 6/8 time

While you count	☐	☐	☐	☐	☐	☐	☐	☐
Tap and switch	☐	☐	☐	☐	☐	☐	☐	☐
Slow motion	☐	☐	☐	☐	☐	☐	☐	☐
Riding the tiger	☐	☐	☐	☐	☐	☐	☐	☐
In sync	☐	☐	☐	☐	☐	☐	☐	☐
From memory	☐	☐	☐	☐	☐	☐	☐	☐
Your tune	☐	☐	☐	☐	☐	☐	☐	☐

Twists   1 ☐   2 ☐   3 ☐   4 ☐   5 ☐   6 ☐   7 ☐   8 ☐   9 ☐   10 ☐

Complete all 56 basic quests to unlock Twists. See the back of the book for Twist instructions.

12 complete — ☐ Trainee

24 complete — ☐ Intermediate

40 complete — ☐ **Level 18 Unlocked**

56 complete — ☐ **Twists Unlocked**

All complete — ☐ Master

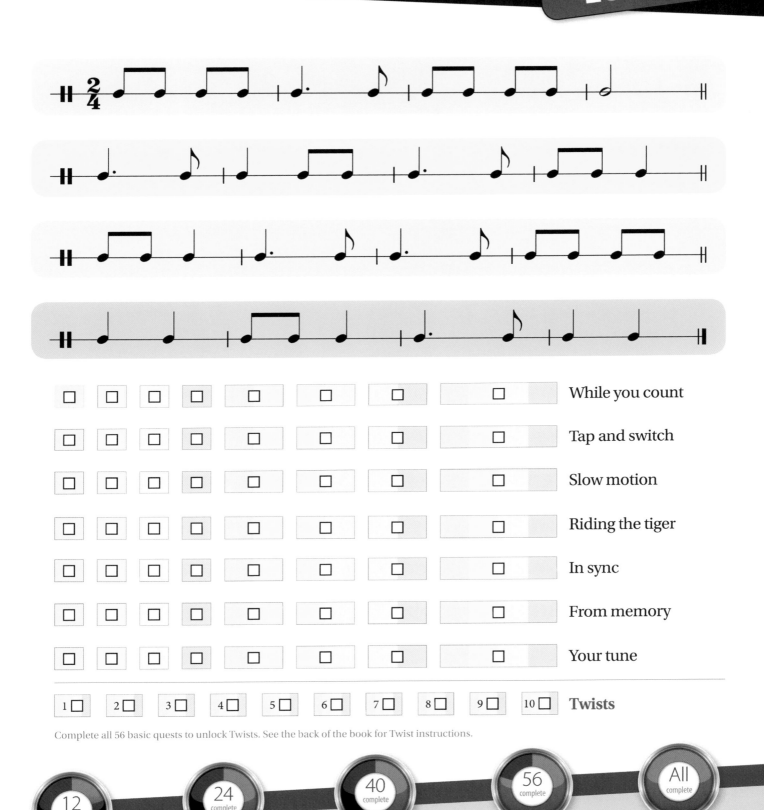

☐	☐	☐	☐	☐	☐	☐	☐	While you count
☐	☐	☐	☐	☐	☐	☐	☐	Tap and switch
☐	☐	☐	☐	☐	☐	☐	☐	Slow motion
☐	☐	☐	☐	☐	☐	☐	☐	Riding the tiger
☐	☐	☐	☐	☐	☐	☐	☐	In sync
☐	☐	☐	☐	☐	☐	☐	☐	From memory
☐	☐	☐	☐	☐	☐	☐	☐	Your tune

1 ☐   2 ☐   3 ☐   4 ☐   5 ☐   6 ☐   7 ☐   8 ☐   9 ☐   10 ☐ **Twists**

Complete all 56 basic quests to unlock Twists. See the back of the book for Twist instructions.

12 complete   **24** complete   **40** complete   **56** complete   **All** complete

☐ Trainee   ☐ Intermediate   ☐ **Level 19 Unlocked**   ☐ Twists Unlocked   ☐ Master

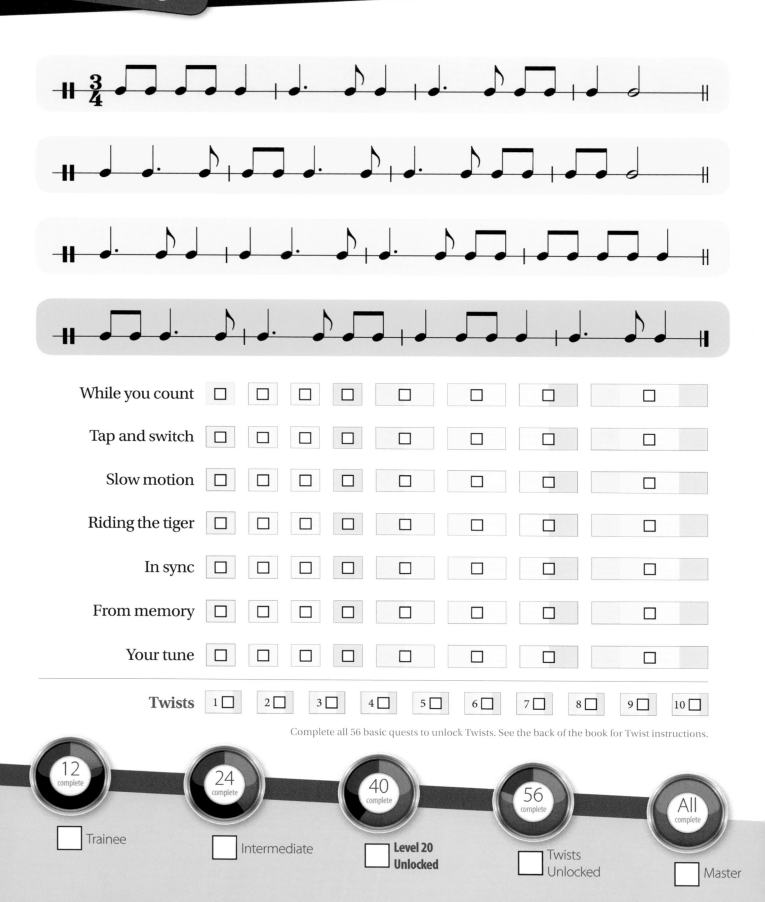

Level 19

New: Dotted quarter notes in 3/4 time

While you count	☐	☐	☐	☐	☐	☐	☐	☐
Tap and switch	☐	☐	☐	☐	☐	☐	☐	☐
Slow motion	☐	☐	☐	☐	☐	☐	☐	☐
Riding the tiger	☐	☐	☐	☐	☐	☐	☐	☐
In sync	☐	☐	☐	☐	☐	☐	☐	☐
From memory	☐	☐	☐	☐	☐	☐	☐	☐
Your tune	☐	☐	☐	☐	☐	☐	☐	☐

Twists 1 ☐ 2 ☐ 3 ☐ 4 ☐ 5 ☐ 6 ☐ 7 ☐ 8 ☐ 9 ☐ 10 ☐

Complete all 56 basic quests to unlock Twists. See the back of the book for Twist instructions.

12 complete — ☐ Trainee

24 complete — ☐ Intermediate

40 complete — ☐ **Level 20 Unlocked**

56 complete — ☐ Twists Unlocked

All complete — ☐ Master

New: Dotted quarter notes in 4/4 time

Level 20

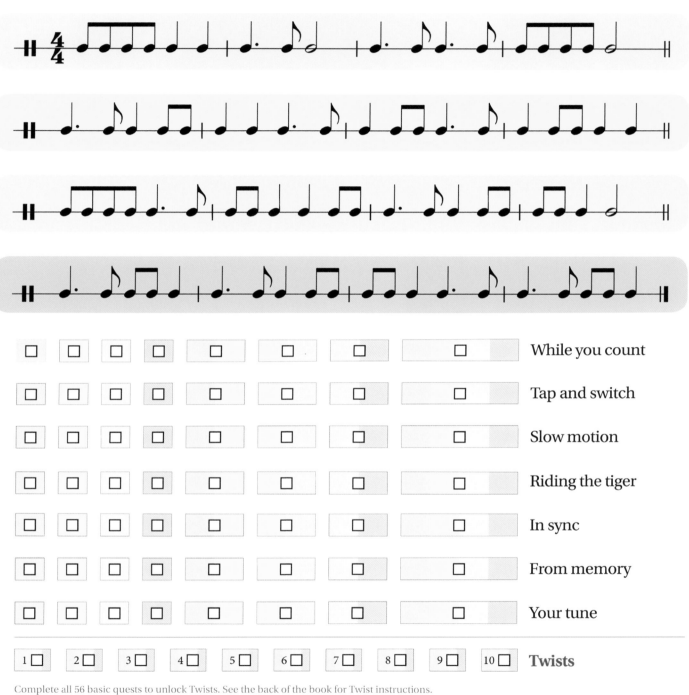

☐	☐	☐	☐	☐	☐	☐	☐	While you count
☐	☐	☐	☐	☐	☐	☐	☐	Tap and switch
☐	☐	☐	☐	☐	☐	☐	☐	Slow motion
☐	☐	☐	☐	☐	☐	☐	☐	Riding the tiger
☐	☐	☐	☐	☐	☐	☐	☐	In sync
☐	☐	☐	☐	☐	☐	☐	☐	From memory
☐	☐	☐	☐	☐	☐	☐	☐	Your tune

1 ☐ 2 ☐ 3 ☐ 4 ☐ 5 ☐ 6 ☐ 7 ☐ 8 ☐ 9 ☐ 10 ☐ **Twists**

Complete all 56 basic quests to unlock Twists. See the back of the book for Twist instructions.

Level 21 New: Eighth note rests

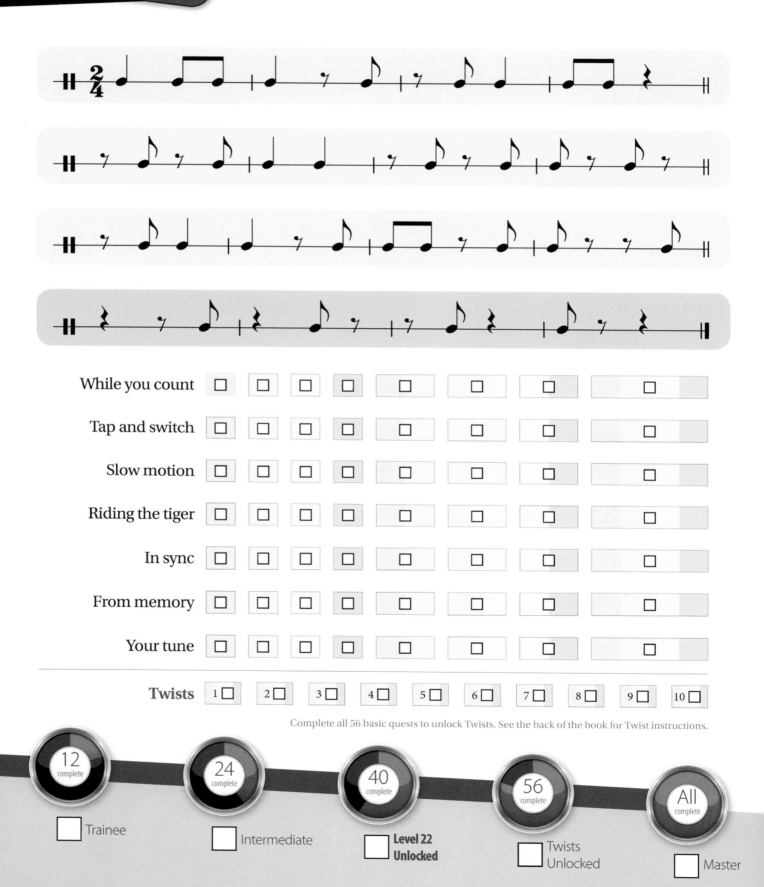

While you count	☐	☐	☐	☐	☐	☐	☐	☐
Tap and switch	☐	☐	☐	☐	☐	☐	☐	☐
Slow motion	☐	☐	☐	☐	☐	☐	☐	☐
Riding the tiger	☐	☐	☐	☐	☐	☐	☐	☐
In sync	☐	☐	☐	☐	☐	☐	☐	☐
From memory	☐	☐	☐	☐	☐	☐	☐	☐
Your tune	☐	☐	☐	☐	☐	☐	☐	☐

Twists 1 ☐ 2 ☐ 3 ☐ 4 ☐ 5 ☐ 6 ☐ 7 ☐ 8 ☐ 9 ☐ 10 ☐

Complete all 56 basic quests to unlock Twists. See the back of the book for Twist instructions.

12 complete

24 complete

40 complete

56 complete

All complete

☐ Trainee ☐ Intermediate ☐ **Level 22 Unlocked** ☐ Twists Unlocked ☐ Master

Level 22

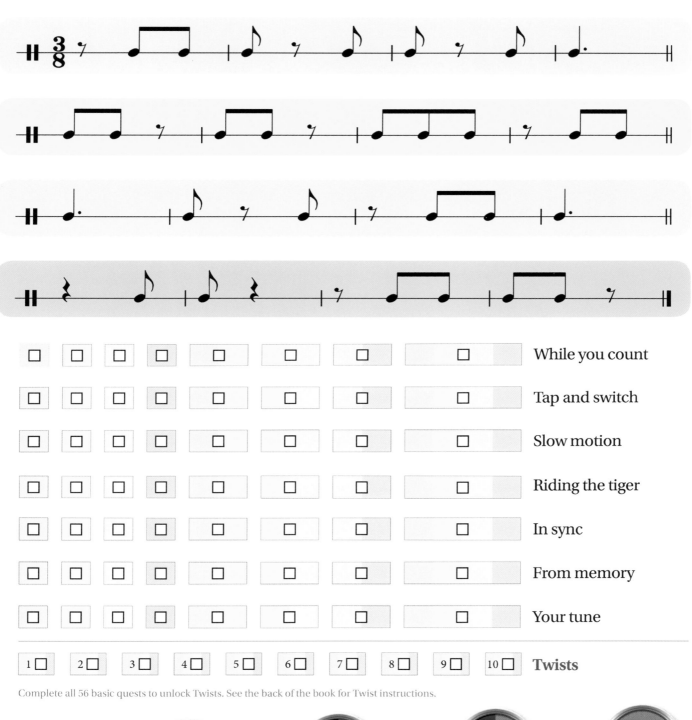

								While you count
☐	☐	☐	☐	☐	☐	☐	☐	While you count
☐	☐	☐	☐	☐	☐	☐	☐	Tap and switch
☐	☐	☐	☐	☐	☐	☐	☐	Slow motion
☐	☐	☐	☐	☐	☐	☐	☐	Riding the tiger
☐	☐	☐	☐	☐	☐	☐	☐	In sync
☐	☐	☐	☐	☐	☐	☐	☐	From memory
☐	☐	☐	☐	☐	☐	☐	☐	Your tune

1 ☐   2 ☐   3 ☐   4 ☐   5 ☐   6 ☐   7 ☐   8 ☐   9 ☐   10 ☐   **Twists**

Complete all 56 basic quests to unlock Twists. See the back of the book for Twist instructions.

12 complete
24 complete
40 complete
56 complete
All complete

☐ Trainee   ☐ Intermediate   ☐ **Level 23 Unlocked**   ☐ Twists Unlocked   ☐ Master

Level 23

New: Eighth note rests in 6/8 time

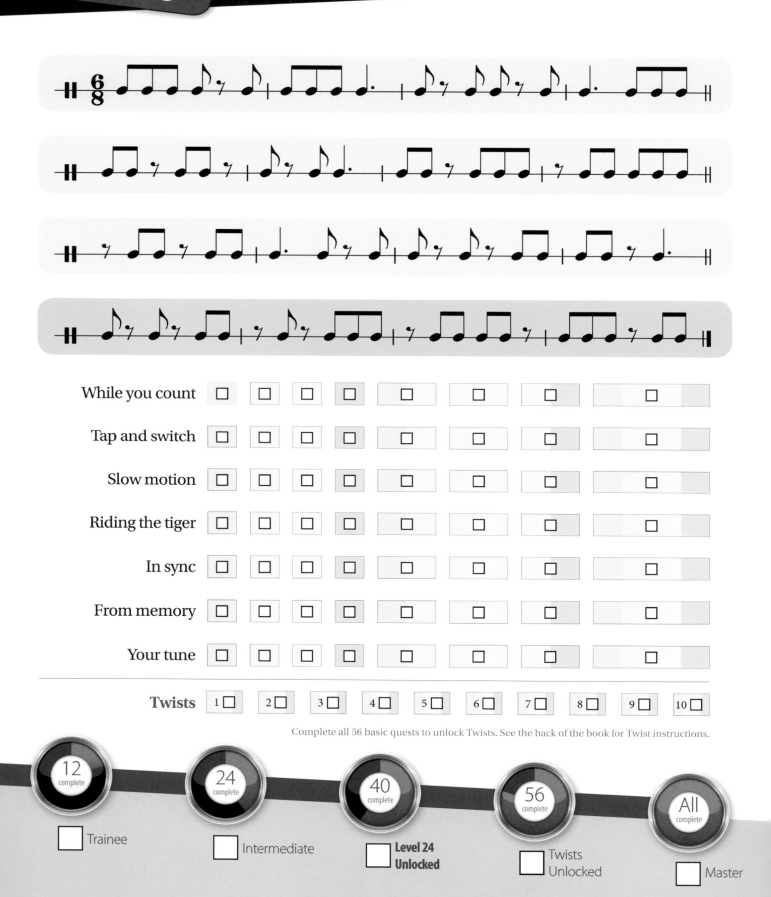

While you count	☐	☐	☐	☐	☐	☐	☐	☐
Tap and switch	☐	☐	☐	☐	☐	☐	☐	☐
Slow motion	☐	☐	☐	☐	☐	☐	☐	☐
Riding the tiger	☐	☐	☐	☐	☐	☐	☐	☐
In sync	☐	☐	☐	☐	☐	☐	☐	☐
From memory	☐	☐	☐	☐	☐	☐	☐	☐
Your tune	☐	☐	☐	☐	☐	☐	☐	☐

Twists 1 ☐ 2 ☐ 3 ☐ 4 ☐ 5 ☐ 6 ☐ 7 ☐ 8 ☐ 9 ☐ 10 ☐

Complete all 56 basic quests to unlock Twists. See the back of the book for Twist instructions.

12 complete ☐ Trainee

24 complete ☐ Intermediate

40 complete ☐ **Level 24 Unlocked**

56 complete ☐ **Twists Unlocked**

All complete ☐ Master

Level 24

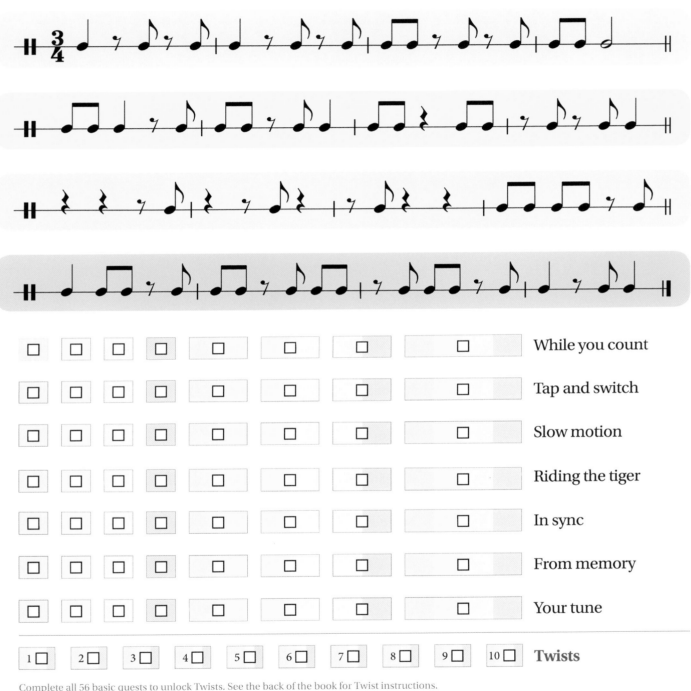

								While you count
☐	☐	☐	☐	☐	☐	☐	☐	While you count
☐	☐	☐	☐	☐	☐	☐	☐	Tap and switch
☐	☐	☐	☐	☐	☐	☐	☐	Slow motion
☐	☐	☐	☐	☐	☐	☐	☐	Riding the tiger
☐	☐	☐	☐	☐	☐	☐	☐	In sync
☐	☐	☐	☐	☐	☐	☐	☐	From memory
☐	☐	☐	☐	☐	☐	☐	☐	Your tune

1 ☐   2 ☐   3 ☐   4 ☐   5 ☐   6 ☐   7 ☐   8 ☐   9 ☐   10 ☐   **Twists**

Complete all 56 basic quests to unlock Twists. See the back of the book for Twist instructions.

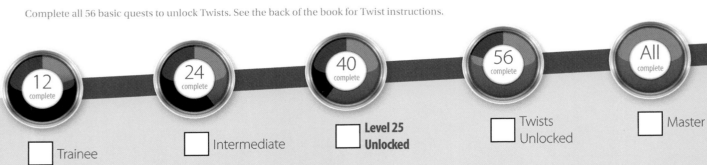

12 complete

24 complete

40 complete

56 complete

All complete

☐ Trainee   ☐ Intermediate   ☐ **Level 25 Unlocked**   ☐ Twists Unlocked   ☐ Master

Level 25

While you count	☐	☐	☐	☐	☐	☐	☐	☐
Tap and switch	☐	☐	☐	☐	☐	☐	☐	☐
Slow motion	☐	☐	☐	☐	☐	☐	☐	☐
Riding the tiger	☐	☐	☐	☐	☐	☐	☐	☐
In sync	☐	☐	☐	☐	☐	☐	☐	☐
From memory	☐	☐	☐	☐	☐	☐	☐	☐
Your tune	☐	☐	☐	☐	☐	☐	☐	☐

Twists 1 ☐ 2 ☐ 3 ☐ 4 ☐ 5 ☐ 6 ☐ 7 ☐ 8 ☐ 9 ☐ 10 ☐

Complete all 56 basic quests to unlock Twists. See the back of the book for Twist instructions.

12 complete	24 complete	40 complete	56 complete	All complete
☐ Trainee	☐ Intermediate	☐ **Level 26 Unlocked**	☐ Twists Unlocked	☐ Master

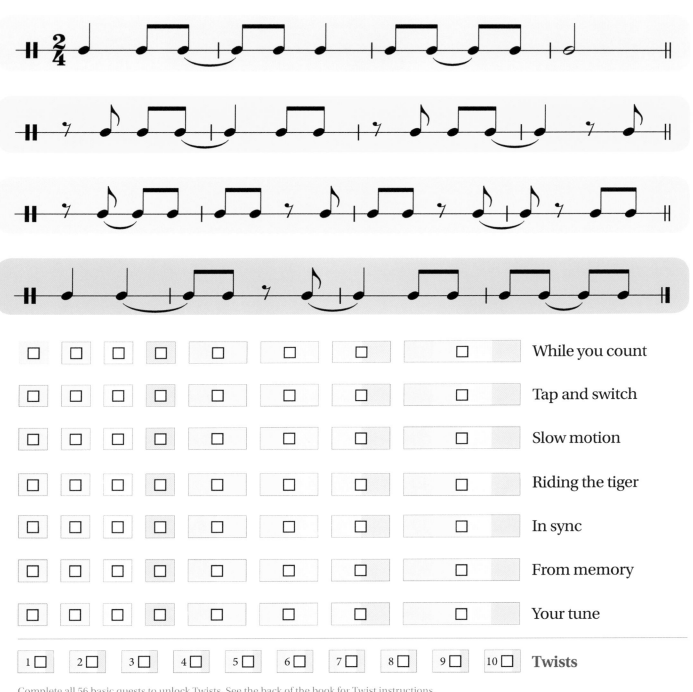

☐	☐	☐	☐	☐	☐	☐	☐	While you count
☐	☐	☐	☐	☐	☐	☐	☐	Tap and switch
☐	☐	☐	☐	☐	☐	☐	☐	Slow motion
☐	☐	☐	☐	☐	☐	☐	☐	Riding the tiger
☐	☐	☐	☐	☐	☐	☐	☐	In sync
☐	☐	☐	☐	☐	☐	☐	☐	From memory
☐	☐	☐	☐	☐	☐	☐	☐	Your tune

1 ☐ 2 ☐ 3 ☐ 4 ☐ 5 ☐ 6 ☐ 7 ☐ 8 ☐ 9 ☐ 10 ☐ **Twists**

Complete all 56 basic quests to unlock Twists. See the back of the book for Twist instructions.

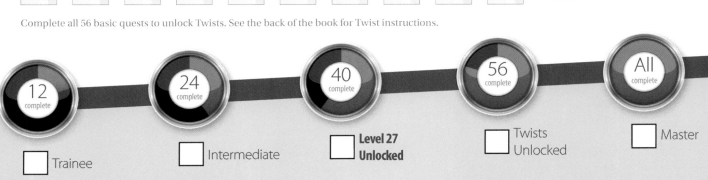

12 complete	24 complete	40 complete	56 complete	All complete
☐ Trainee	☐ Intermediate	☐ **Level 27 Unlocked**	☐ Twists Unlocked	☐ Master

Level 27

New: Tied eighth notes in 3/8 time

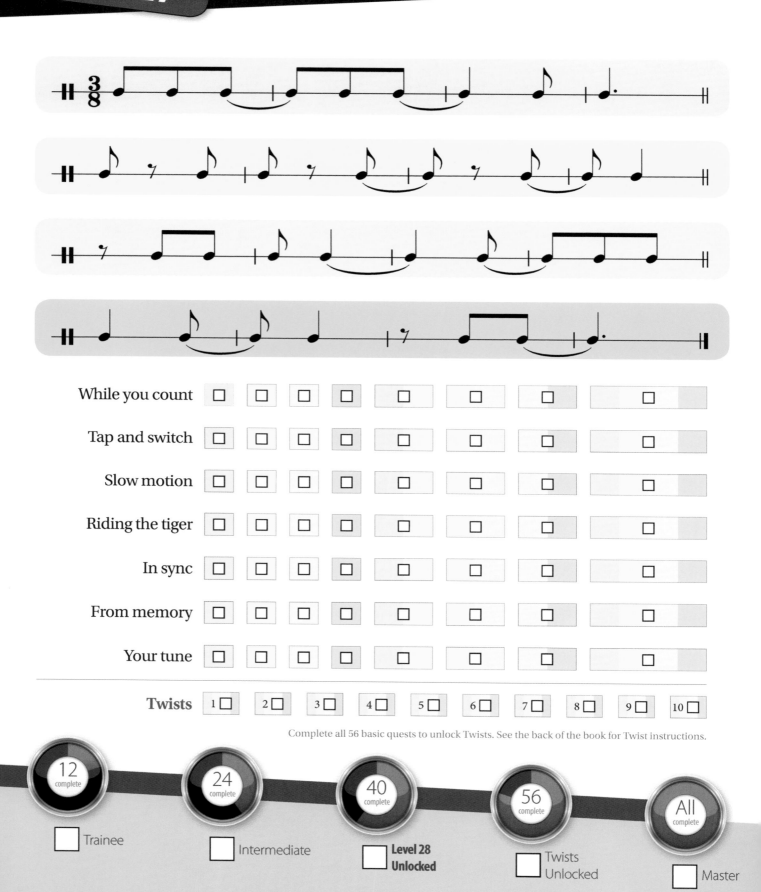

While you count	☐	☐	☐	☐	☐	☐	☐	☐
Tap and switch	☐	☐	☐	☐	☐	☐	☐	☐
Slow motion	☐	☐	☐	☐	☐	☐	☐	☐
Riding the tiger	☐	☐	☐	☐	☐	☐	☐	☐
In sync	☐	☐	☐	☐	☐	☐	☐	☐
From memory	☐	☐	☐	☐	☐	☐	☐	☐
Your tune	☐	☐	☐	☐	☐	☐	☐	☐

Twists   1 ☐   2 ☐   3 ☐   4 ☐   5 ☐   6 ☐   7 ☐   8 ☐   9 ☐   10 ☐

Complete all 56 basic quests to unlock Twists. See the back of the book for Twist instructions.

12 complete

24 complete

40 complete

56 complete

All complete

☐ Trainee

☐ Intermediate

☐ **Level 28 Unlocked**

☐ Twists Unlocked

☐ Master

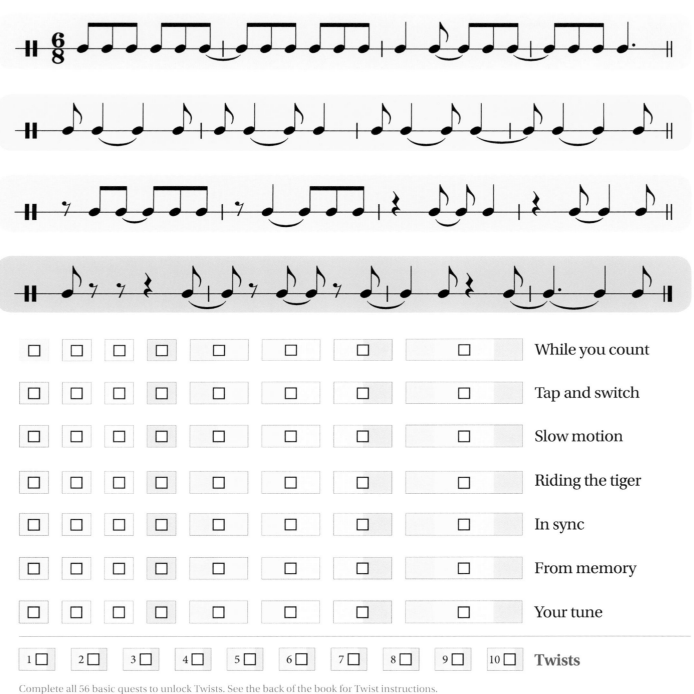

								While you count
☐	☐	☐	☐	☐	☐	☐	☐	While you count
☐	☐	☐	☐	☐	☐	☐	☐	Tap and switch
☐	☐	☐	☐	☐	☐	☐	☐	Slow motion
☐	☐	☐	☐	☐	☐	☐	☐	Riding the tiger
☐	☐	☐	☐	☐	☐	☐	☐	In sync
☐	☐	☐	☐	☐	☐	☐	☐	From memory
☐	☐	☐	☐	☐	☐	☐	☐	Your tune

1 ☐ 2 ☐ 3 ☐ 4 ☐ 5 ☐ 6 ☐ 7 ☐ 8 ☐ 9 ☐ 10 ☐ **Twists**

Complete all 56 basic quests to unlock Twists. See the back of the book for Twist instructions.

12 complete

24 complete

40 complete

56 complete

All complete

☐ Trainee ☐ Intermediate ☐ **Level 29 Unlocked** ☐ Twists Unlocked ☐ Master

Level 29

New: Tied eighth notes in 3/4 time

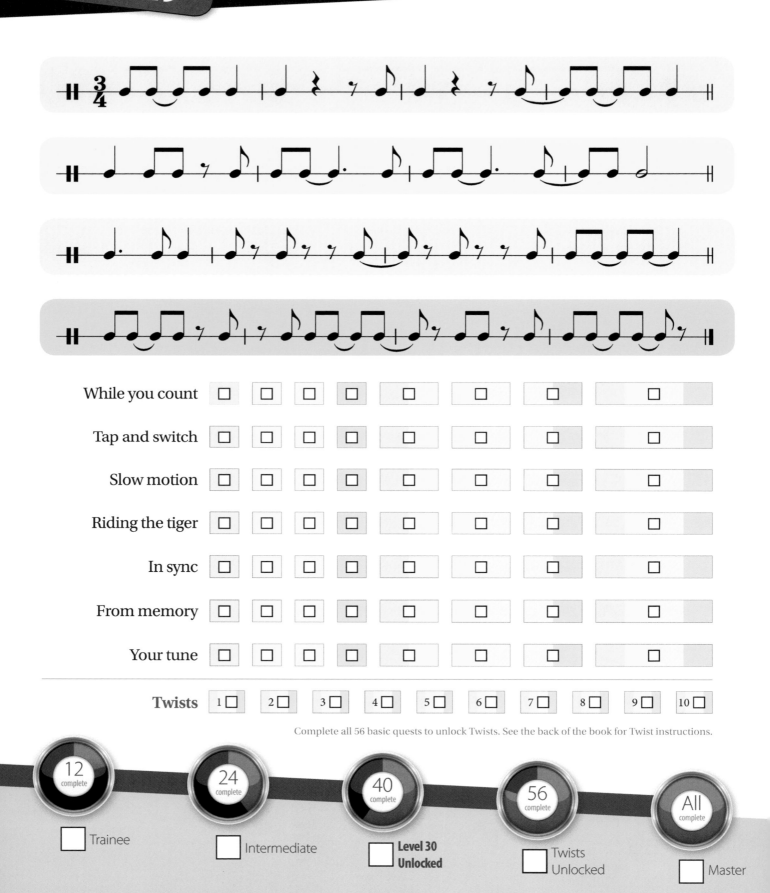

While you count	☐	☐	☐	☐	☐	☐	☐	☐
Tap and switch	☐	☐	☐	☐	☐	☐	☐	☐
Slow motion	☐	☐	☐	☐	☐	☐	☐	☐
Riding the tiger	☐	☐	☐	☐	☐	☐	☐	☐
In sync	☐	☐	☐	☐	☐	☐	☐	☐
From memory	☐	☐	☐	☐	☐	☐	☐	☐
Your tune	☐	☐	☐	☐	☐	☐	☐	☐

Twists 1 ☐ 2 ☐ 3 ☐ 4 ☐ 5 ☐ 6 ☐ 7 ☐ 8 ☐ 9 ☐ 10 ☐

Complete all 56 basic quests to unlock Twists. See the back of the book for Twist instructions.

12 complete

24 complete

40 complete

56 complete

All complete

☐ Trainee

☐ Intermediate

☐ **Level 30 Unlocked**

☐ **Twists Unlocked**

☐ Master

☐	☐	☐	☐	☐	☐	☐	☐	While you count
☐	☐	☐	☐	☐	☐	☐	☐	Tap and switch
☐	☐	☐	☐	☐	☐	☐	☐	Slow motion
☐	☐	☐	☐	☐	☐	☐	☐	Riding the tiger
☐	☐	☐	☐	☐	☐	☐	☐	In sync
☐	☐	☐	☐	☐	☐	☐	☐	From memory
☐	☐	☐	☐	☐	☐	☐	☐	Your tune

1 ☐ 2 ☐ 3 ☐ 4 ☐ 5 ☐ 6 ☐ 7 ☐ 8 ☐ 9 ☐ 10 ☐ **Twists**

Complete all 56 basic quests to unlock Twists. See the back of the book for Twist instructions.

12 complete — Trainee

24 complete — Intermediate

40 complete — **Level 31 Unlocked**

56 complete — Twists Unlocked

All complete — Master

Level 31

New: Chaotic rests

While you count	☐	☐	☐	☐	☐	☐	☐	☐
Tap and switch	☐	☐	☐	☐	☐	☐	☐	☐
Slow motion	☐	☐	☐	☐	☐	☐	☐	☐
Riding the tiger	☐	☐	☐	☐	☐	☐	☐	☐
In sync	☐	☐	☐	☐	☐	☐	☐	☐
From memory	☐	☐	☐	☐	☐	☐	☐	☐
Your tune	☐	☐	☐	☐	☐	☐	☐	☐

Twists   1 ☐   2 ☐   3 ☐   4 ☐   5 ☐   6 ☐   7 ☐   8 ☐   9 ☐   10 ☐

Complete all 56 basic quests to unlock Twists. See the back of the book for Twist instructions.

12 complete — Trainee

24 complete — Intermediate

40 complete — **Level 32 Unlocked**

56 complete — Twists Unlocked

All complete — Master

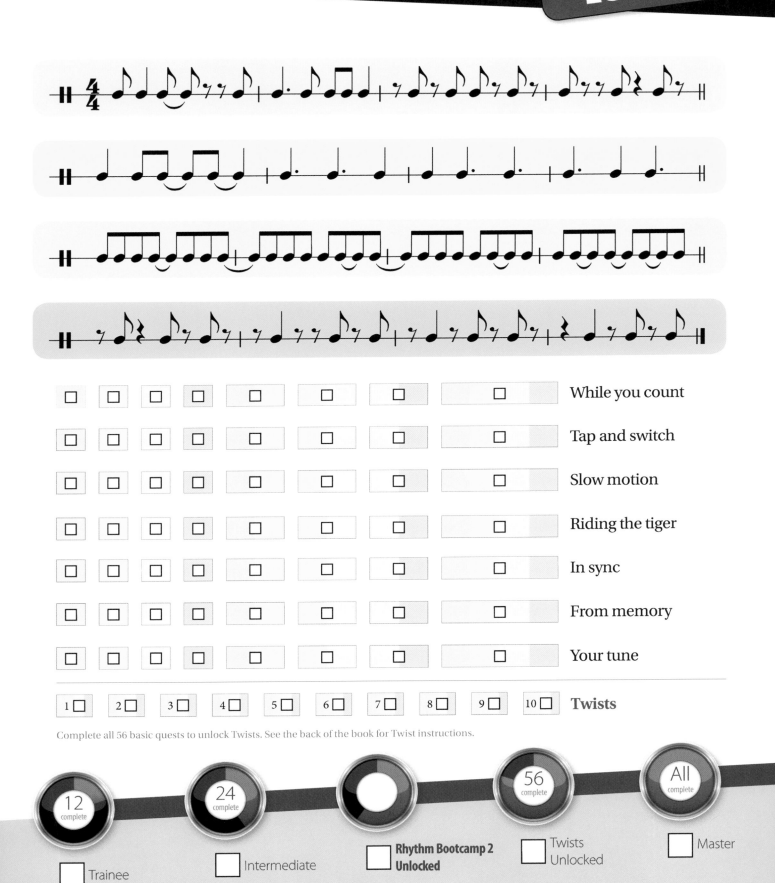

								While you count
☐	☐	☐	☐	☐	☐	☐	☐	**Tap and switch**
☐	☐	☐	☐	☐	☐	☐	☐	**Slow motion**
☐	☐	☐	☐	☐	☐	☐	☐	**Riding the tiger**
☐	☐	☐	☐	☐	☐	☐	☐	**In sync**
☐	☐	☐	☐	☐	☐	☐	☐	**From memory**
☐	☐	☐	☐	☐	☐	☐	☐	**Your tune**

1 ☐   2 ☐   3 ☐   4 ☐   5 ☐   6 ☐   7 ☐   8 ☐   9 ☐   10 ☐   **Twists**

Complete all 56 basic quests to unlock Twists. See the back of the book for Twist instructions.

12 complete   **24** complete   ○   **56** complete   **All** complete

☐ Trainee   ☐ Intermediate   ☐ **Rhythm Bootcamp 2 Unlocked**   ☐ Twists Unlocked   ☐ Master

Twist 1: Your lyrics.

① Write whatever words you like under the rhythm, making sure each syllable lines up with a single note.

② Practice until you can say your lyrics correctly with the given rhythm. Tempo is up to you.

❗ There's no rule that says the lyrics have to make sense. (The example below doesn't. Stop trying to analyse it.)

Example:

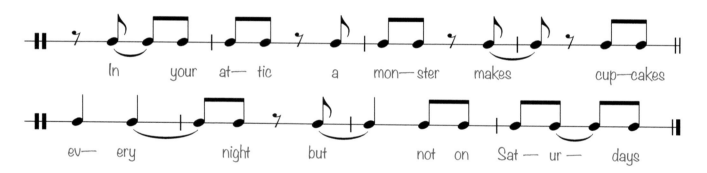

In your at— tic   a   mon—ster   makes   cup—cakes

ev— ery   night   but   not on Sat — ur — days

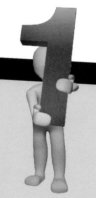

Track your progress: Which levels have you completed this twist for?

1 2 3 4 5 6 7 8 9 10 11 12 13 14 15 16
☐ ☐ ☐ ☐ ☐ ☐ ☐ ☐ ☐ ☐ ☐ ☐ ☐ ☐ ☐ ☐

17 18 19 20 21 22 23 24 25 26 27 28 29 30 31 32
☐ ☐ ☐ ☐ ☐ ☐ ☐ ☐ ☐ ☐ ☐ ☐ ☐ ☐ ☐ ☐

Twist 2: Hear it. Write it.

① Have your teacher play the rhythm to you, or listen to the recording online (see below).

② Write out the rhythm correctly on a blank sheet of manuscript paper, just by hearing it.

! You can listen to each rhythm—or any part of each rhythm—as many times as you need to while you figure this out.

Listen online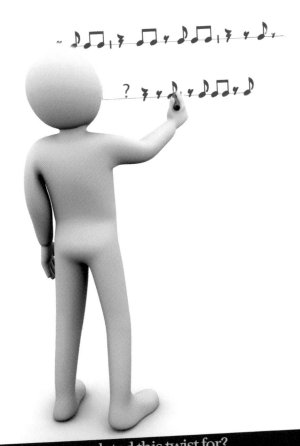

You can listen to recordings of each rhythm at www.insidemusicteaching.com (in the Rhythm Bootcamp section)

Track your progress: Which levels have you completed this twist for?

1	2	3	4	5	6	7	8	9	10	11	12	13	14	15	16
☐	☐	☐	☐	☐	☐	☐	☐	☐	☐	☐	☐	☐	☐	☐	☐

17	18	19	20	21	22	23	24	25	26	27	28	29	30	31	32
☐	☐	☐	☐	☐	☐	☐	☐	☐	☐	☐	☐	☐	☐	☐	☐

Twist 3: A Sometimes Metronome.

① Set your metronome to whatever tempo you like...but make sure it only ticks at the **start** of each measure.

② Play the rhythm from beginning to end correctly, without drifting from the metronome.

❗ You'll need to keep your rhythm tight—and your tempo under control—to have any chance of staying in sync.

Example:

Track your progress: Which levels have you completed this twist for?

1 2 3 4 5 6 7 8 9 10 11 12 13 14 15 16
☐ ☐ ☐ ☐ ☐ ☐ ☐ ☐ ☐ ☐ ☐ ☐ ☐ ☐ ☐ ☐

17 18 19 20 21 22 23 24 25 26 27 28 29 30 31 32
☐ ☐ ☐ ☐ ☐ ☐ ☐ ☐ ☐ ☐ ☐ ☐ ☐ ☐ ☐ ☐

Twist 4: One measure on. One measure off.

① Play the rhythm as written...but with a full measure's rest inserted at the end of every measure.

❗ If a tie goes across a barline, simply hold the note through the new empty measure.

Example: - instead of:

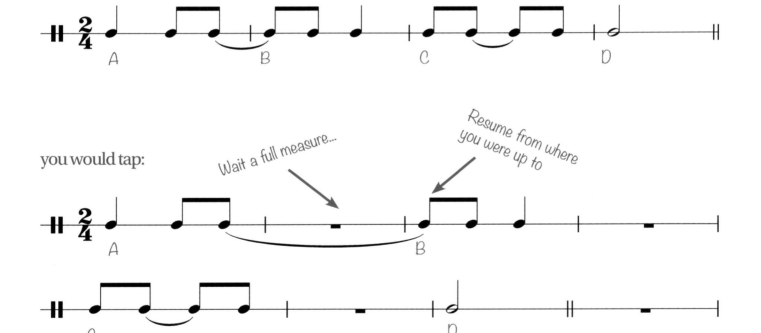

you would tap:

Wait a full measure...

Resume from where you were up to

Track your progress: Which levels have you completed this twist for?

1 2 3 4 5 6 7 8 9 10 11 12 13 14 15 16

17 18 19 20 21 22 23 24 25 26 27 28 29 30 31 32

Twist 5: Scat that.

① Improvise your own nonsense syllables as you say the rhythm.

! Unlike *With Lyrics* (Twist 1), you don't get to write these syllables out in advance. The whole point is to be *improvising* your nonsense syllables, and for your brain to be busy with exactly that...which means it can't be busy trying to figure out the rhythm. You have to know it.

Example:

etc.

Track your progress: Which levels have you completed this twist for?

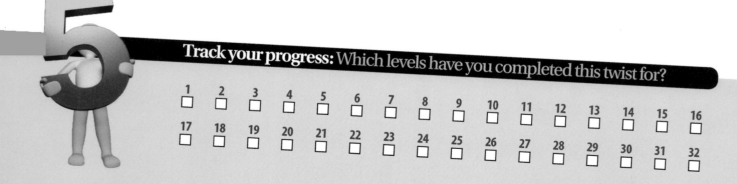

Twist 6: Your dynamics.

① Write in your own dynamic markings—at least 8—then perform the rhythm observing those dynamics.

! Don't worry about creating musically sensible dynamics—aim for plenty of variety and chaotic changes. So not so much a pleasant car journey through the hills as a Roller Coaster Of Dynamic Disorientation.

Example:

Track your progress: Which levels have you completed this twist for?

1	2	3	4	5	6	7	8	9	10	11	12	13	14	15	16
☐	☐	☐	☐	☐	☐	☐	☐	☐	☐	☐	☐	☐	☐	☐	☐

17	18	19	20	21	22	23	24	25	26	27	28	29	30	31	32
☐	☐	☐	☐	☐	☐	☐	☐	☐	☐	☐	☐	☐	☐	☐	☐

Twist 7: Insane accents.

① Mark in at least 8 different accents, then perform the rhythm observing those accents.

❗ Avoid placing your accents neatly on the first beat of each measure...your job is to really mix them up, so they're popping in the most unexpected—and inconvenient—of locations. (It wouldn't be a Twist if it was straightforward).

Example: Not nice and tidy like this...

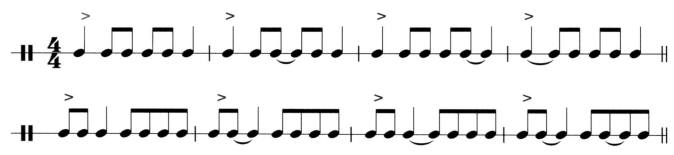

...but completely nuts, like this. (Try it!)

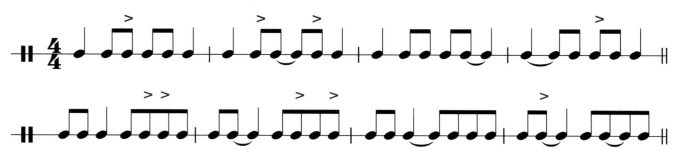

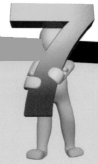

Track your progress: Which levels have you completed this twist for?

1	2	3	4	5	6	7	8	9	10	11	12	13	14	15	16
☐	☐	☐	☐	☐	☐	☐	☐	☐	☐	☐	☐	☐	☐	☐	☐

17	18	19	20	21	22	23	24	25	26	27	28	29	30	31	32
☐	☐	☐	☐	☐	☐	☐	☐	☐	☐	☐	☐	☐	☐	☐	☐

Twist 8: Runaway train.

① Tap the rhythm, but gradually speed up as you do. You should end up around twice as fast as your starting speed.

❗ Conventional metronomes won't help, but there's a free online Runaway Train metronome at insidemusicteaching.com that goes from 80bpm to 150 over 16 measures...strap in and hang on...

Example: (The approximate speeds from the *Runaway train* free online metronome)

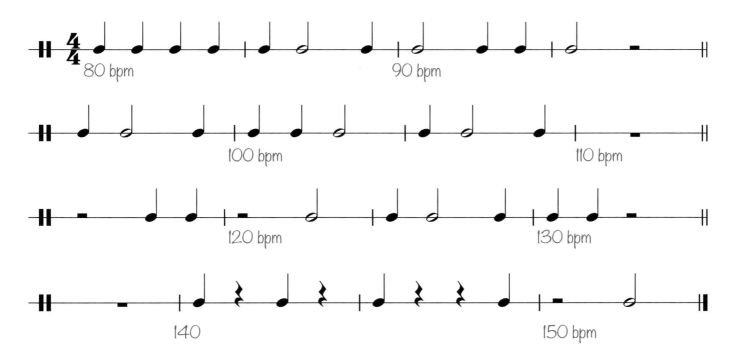

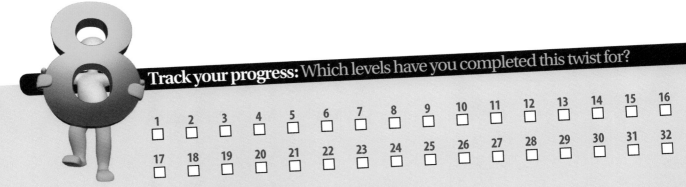

Track your progress: Which levels have you completed this twist for?

1 2 3 4 5 6 7 8 9 10 11 12 13 14 15 16

17 18 19 20 21 22 23 24 25 26 27 28 29 30 31 32

Twist 9: Runaway train...up a hill.

① Tap the rhythm, but gradually slow down as you do. You should end up around half as fast as your starting speed.

❗ Again, there's a special metronome at insidemusicteaching.com that starts at 150 bpm, then gradually slows down to 80 bpm over 16 measures.

Example: (The approximate speeds from the *Runaway train...up a hill* online metronome)

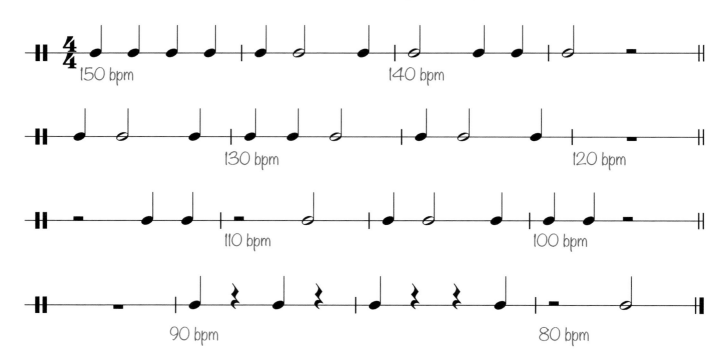

Track your progress: Which levels have you completed this twist for?

1	2	3	4	5	6	7	8	9	10	11	12	13	14	15	16
☐	☐	☐	☐	☐	☐	☐	☐	☐	☐	☐	☐	☐	☐	☐	☐

17	18	19	20	21	22	23	24	25	26	27	28	29	30	31	32
☐	☐	☐	☐	☐	☐	☐	☐	☐	☐	☐	☐	☐	☐	☐	☐

Twist 10: Mirrored.

① Reading from the last note of the rhythm backwards, write out the mirrored version of the rhythm.

② Tap the mirrored rhythm correctly.

! Check your written out version carefully. Recordings of the reversed rhythms are available at insidemusicteaching.com.

Original Rhythm:

Written out reversed:

Track your progress: Which levels have you completed this twist for?

| 1 | 2 | 3 | 4 | 5 | 6 | 7 | 8 | 9 | 10 | 11 | 12 | 13 | 14 | 15 | 16 |

| 17 | 18 | 19 | 20 | 21 | 22 | 23 | 24 | 25 | 26 | 27 | 28 | 29 | 30 | 31 | 32 |

Scales Bootcamp

You've never seen a scales manual like this. Super-clear layout to help students figure out scales fast, with an insane variety of practice challenges and twists, keeping scales practice fresh, unpredictable and strangely compelling.

The promise: Earn all the listed achievements for any scale in the book, and you'll know that scale permanently...whether you practice it ever again or not(!)

View the movie tours at insidemusicteaching.com

The Dynamic Studio

Philip Johnston's most acclaimed book outlines more ideas to try than any one teacher would ever get through in a lifetime.

From motivation systems to resourcing, repertoire selection to the practice treadmill, unconventional scheduling to simply how to make a studio more fun, *The Dynamic Studio* is another explosion of possibilities from the world's best known writer on music teaching.

More information at insidemusicteaching.com

Rhythm Bootcamp 2

The next 32 Levels of the Rhythm Bootcamp adventure, with tougher challenges including sixteenth notes, complex and additive time signatures, tuplets and more.

For intermediate to advanced students who are serious about permanently transforming their rhythm reading skills, and the perfect follow up for graduates of Rhythm Bootcamp 1.

More information at insidemusicteaching.com

Practiceopedia

The largest guide to practicing ever assembled—a massive 376 color illustrated pages of cross-referenced practice ideas, tips, tricks and traps.

"The ultimate reference for students...this is a 'must have' book. Practicing will be a brand new game every time."
Music Teacher International

View the movie tours at insidemusicteaching.com

www.**inside**music**teaching**.com

CPSIA information can be obtained
at www.ICGtesting.com
Printed in the USA
LVIC04n0610250516
489878LV00005B/33